Read for a Better World™

MAKING FRIENDS AT SCHOOL

MARGO GATES

GRL Consultants,
Diane Craig and Monica Marx,
Certified Literacy Specialists

Lerner Publications ◆ Minneapolis

Educator Toolbox

Reading books is a great way for kids to express what they're interested in. Before reading this title, ask the reader these questions:

> What do you think this book is about? Look at the cover for clues.

> What do you already know about making friends at school?

> What do you want to find out about making friends at school?

Let's Read Together

Encourage the reader to use the pictures to understand the text.

Point out when the reader successfully sounds out a word.

Praise the reader for recognizing sight words such as *make* and *you*.

TABLE OF CONTENTS

Making Friends at School. . . 4

Making Friends at School

You go to school
to learn.
You make friends
at school too!

A friend is
someone you
like to be with.
Friends care
about each other.

Do you have a friend you care about?

You make friends
by being kind.
Say hello to a
classmate.

You make friends by
asking questions.

Find out what your classmate likes.

You and your classmates may like different things.
But you can still be friends.

Do you and your friend like different things?

You may have
a good friend.
But you can be
friends with more
than one person.

Have lunch with classmates you don't know well.

At recess, let everyone play and have fun.

Say goodbye to your friends after school. You will see them tomorrow!

You Connect!

Who is a friend you like to be with?

What do you like about your friend?

What do you do to be a good friend?

Social and Emotional Snapshot

Student voice is crucial to building reader confidence. Ask the reader:

What is your favorite part of this book?

What is something you learned from this book?

Did this book remind you of your own friends?

Opportunities for social and emotional learning are everywhere. How can you connect the topic of this book to the SEL competencies below?

Self-Awareness
Relationship Skills
Social Awareness

Photo Glossary

classmate

friends

lunch

recess

Learn More

Berube, Kate. *Mae's First Day of School*. New York: Abrams Books for Young Readers, 2022.

Gates, Margo. *School Recess*. Minneapolis: Lerner Publications, 2023.

Rustad, Martha E. H. *Michael Makes Friends at School*. Minneapolis: Millbrook Press, 2018.

Index

Photo Acknowledgments

The images in this book are used with the permission of: © Darrin Henry/Shutterstock Images, pp. 14–15; © Jeanette Virginia Goh/Shutterstock Images, pp. 4–5; © mangpor2004/Shutterstock Images, pp. 11, 23 (classmate); © Monkey Business Images/Shutterstock Images, pp. 16–17, 23 (lunch); © Odua Images/Shutterstock Images, pp. 6–7, 23 (friends); © Pressmaster/Shutterstock Images, p. 8; © Ridofranz/iStockphoto, p. 10; © Roman Samborskyi/Shutterstock Images, pp. 12–13; © SDI Productions/iStockphoto, pp. 8–9; © wavebreakmedia/Shutterstock Images, pp. 18–19, 20, 23 (recess).

Cover Photo: FatCamera/iStockphoto.

Design Elements: © Mighty Media, Inc.

Lerner Publications Company
An imprint of Lerner Publishing Group, Inc.
241 First Avenue North
Minneapolis, MN 55401 USA

For reading levels and more information, look up this title at www.lernerbooks.com.

Main body text set in Mikado a Medium.
Typeface provided by Hannes von Doehren.

Library of Congress Cataloging-in-Publication Data

Names: Gates, Margo, author.
Title: Making friends at school / Margo Gates.
Description: Minneapolis, MN : Lerner Publications , [2023] | Series: Read about school (Read for a Better World) | Audience: Ages 5–8 years | Audience: Grades K–1 | Summary: "How to make friends is one of the most daunting parts of school for young students. With strategies for meeting new people, and kid-friendly reflection questions, this book is an excellent choice for beginning learners"– Provided by publisher.
Identifiers: LCCN 2021043617 (print) | LCCN 2021043618 (ebook) | ISBN 9781728459318 (Library Binding) | ISBN 9781728464220 (Paperback) | ISBN 9781728461816 (eBook)
Subjects: LCSH: Schools—Juvenile literature. | Friendship in children—Juvenile literature. | Interpersonal relations in children—Juvenile literature.
Classification: LCC LB1513 .G38 2023 (print) | LCC LB1513 (ebook) | DDC 371—dc23/eng/20211213

LC record available at https://lccn.loc.gov/2021043617
LC ebook record available at https://lccn.loc.gov/2021043618

Manufactured in the United States of America
1 – CG – 7/15/22